Woodpeckers

A Carolrhoda Nature Watch Book

by Cherie Winner

Carolrhoda Books, Inc. / Minneapolis

To Martha Christensen, with deepest thanks for her laughter, her strength of purpose, and her cheerful encouragement.

Special thanks to Dr. Jerry Jackson of Florida Gulf Coast University, Ft. Meyers, Florida, for sharing his time and expertise; and to Dr. Danny Ingold of Muskingum College, New Concord, Ohio, for his helpful review of the manuscript.

Carolrhoda Books, Inc.
A division of Lerner Publishing Group
241 First Avenue North
Minneapolis, MN 55401 U.S.A.

Website address: www.lernerbooks.com

LIBRARY OF CONGRESS CATALOGING-IN-PUBLICATION DATA

Winner, Cherie
  Woodpeckers / by Cherie Winner.
      p.   cm — (A Carolrhoda nature watch book)
  Includes index.
  Summary: Describes the physical characteristics, life cycle, and behaviors of many species of woodpeckers found throughout the world; also discusses some of the threats to their survival.
      ISBN 1–57505–445–0 (lib.bdg.: alk. paper)
      1.Woodpeckers—Juvenile literature. [1. Woodpeckers.
  2. Birds.] I. Title. II. Series
  QL696.P56.W56   2001
  595.3'84—dc21   99–006894

Manufactured in the United States of America
1 2 3 4 5 6 – JR – 06 05 04 03 02 01

CONTENTS

KNOCK KNOCK—
WHO'S THERE?

"Tap, tap, tap—trrrrrrrrrr—tap-tap."
Whenever you're in the woods and you hear that fast, loud, tapping, you know there's a woodpecker nearby. Whether they are looking for insects to eat, building a nest, or just telling the world where they are, all woodpeckers do one thing that very few other birds do: they hammer on trees with their long, strong bills.

Woodpeckers also hammer on people's property—on houses, chimneys, and power poles. They can punch holes in roofs and topple telephone poles. But woodpeckers help people and their wild neighbors, too. They provide holes in which dozens of other creatures, from bees to owls, make their homes. They devour many of the insects that would otherwise destroy lumber and fruit crops. They even eat termites and carpenter ants, insects that could damage a wooden house far more than a drumming woodpecker could.

Woodpeckers sometimes knock on human-made structures such as houses, roofs, and rainspouts. This pileated woodpecker is beating on a telephone pole.

Male and female hairy woodpeckers are easy to tell apart. Males (above) have a red patch on their heads while females (left) do not.

These strong, energetic birds are easy to spot even when they are not tapping on trees. Most of the woodpeckers in North America are black and white. In other places around the world, they are often brown, green, yellow, or rust colored. Most woodpeckers, no matter where they live, have a "ladder" pattern of stripes on their backs. Most also have a splash of red or yellow on their chin, cheek, forehead, or neck. In some species, these bright patches help woodpeckers tell whether another woodpecker is male or female. The male usually has an extra patch of color that the female does not have.

Most woodpeckers, such as the Gila woodpecker (main) *and the greater spotted woodpecker* (inset) *have chunky bodies and short, broad wings. They make a wavy up-and-down path as they fly.*

Woodpeckers are easy to recognize when they fly. They beat their wings a few times, then fold them in next to their bodies and coast a bit before flapping again. When they flap, they rise in the air slightly. When they coast, they drop slightly. As a result, they follow a wavy up-and-down path when they fly.

Woodpeckers belong to a family of birds called **Picidae** (PY-sih-dee). This name comes from the Latin word *picus*, which simply means "woodpecker." Experts think woodpeckers first appeared 50 to 60 million years ago. Their early ancestors probably resembled birds called wrynecks, which today live in parts of Africa, Europe, and Asia. Wrynecks got their name from the way they twist their necks when they become frightened.

There are about 182 **species,** or kinds, of woodpeckers. The list includes birds called flickers (genus *Colaptes*) and sapsuckers (genus *Sphyrapicus*), as well as those commonly called woodpeckers. Twenty-one species live in North America. The others live in South America, Asia, Europe, and Africa. Woodpeckers do not live in the areas around the north and south poles, Australia, New Zealand, New Guinea, Madagascar, or islands in the South Pacific.

White woodpeckers (Melanerpes candidus) *live in South America.*

Distribution of Selected North American Woodpeckers

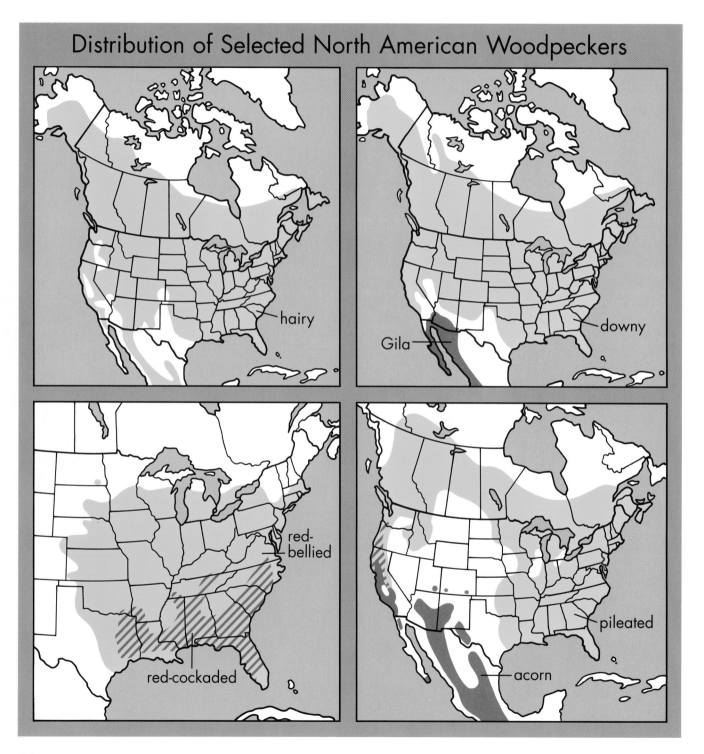

Some woodpeckers live in **habitats,** or environments, with few trees, such as deserts or prairies. But most woodpeckers live in forests where they search for food, chisel holes in trees in which to live, and tap to their heart's content.

Most species of woodpeckers live alone or with their mates all year round. A few species live in larger groups called **colonies.** Each colony may include 10 or more woodpeckers.

If they can find enough food to make it through the winter, most woodpeckers, like the hairy woodpecker pictured above, stay in their homes all year round.

Acorn woodpeckers (left) *live in colonies of about 15 members. They live near one another and search for acorns together.*

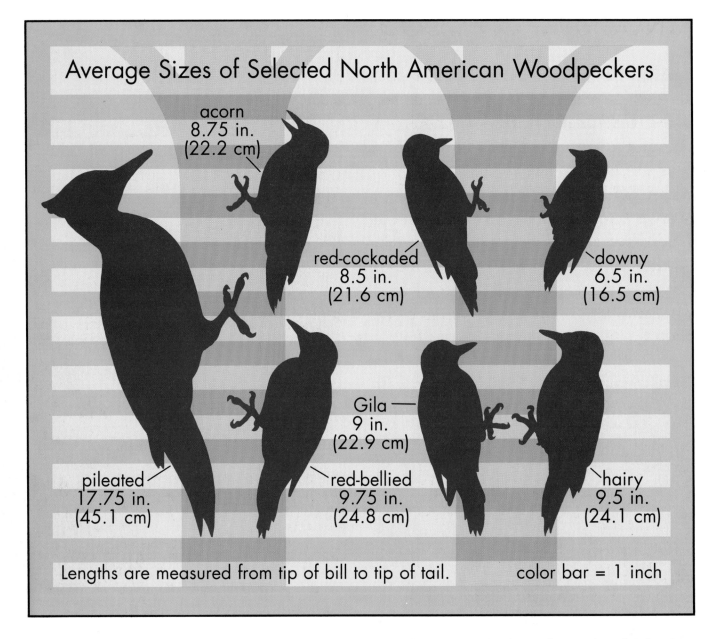

Average Sizes of Selected North American Woodpeckers

acorn
8.75 in.
(22.2 cm)

red-cockaded
8.5 in.
(21.6 cm)

downy
6.5 in.
(16.5 cm)

Gila
9 in.
(22.9 cm)

pileated
17.75 in.
(45.1 cm)

red-bellied
9.75 in.
(24.8 cm)

hairy
9.5 in.
(24.1 cm)

Lengths are measured from tip of bill to tip of tail.   color bar = 1 inch

Woodpeckers come in many sizes. The brown-capped woodpecker *(Picoides moluccensis),* which lives in southern Asia, is only about 3.5 inches (8.9 cm) long and weighs less than an ounce (28 g). The great slaty woodpecker *(Mulleripicus pulverulentus),* which also lives in southern Asia, grows to about 2 feet (60 cm) long and weighs 1.25 pounds (568 g). Most woodpeckers are between 7 and 10 inches (18–25 cm) long.

KNOCKING ON WOOD

Although woodpeckers vary in size, they all have **adaptations,** or special features, that enable them to knock on wood. Woodpeckers use their strong tails to brace themselves against trees as they hammer away. Their short legs, strong toes, and sharp claws help them hold on to the tree trunk as they work. Almost all species have two toes that point forward and two toes that point backward or to the side to enable the birds to cling to the tree.

Different species of woodpeckers hammer in different ways. Yellow-bellied sapsuckers (above) *hold their bodies close to the trunk of a tree, with their legs folded up along the trunk. The birds hit the wood by moving just their heads and necks. Other species put more of their bodies into the work. Black-backed woodpeckers* (left) *stand with their bodies away from the trunk, and use their whole body to hammer away at the wood.*

Since woodpeckers, like this acorn woodpecker, are so strong and hammer so hard, they can cause a lot of damage to human-made structures like telephone poles.

Woodpeckers have muscles that are much stronger than those of most other birds, especially around the tail, chest, and neck. The vertebrae (VUR-tuh-bray), or bones in their spine, are heavier than those in most other birds. These bones provide strong places to which the large muscles are attached. These bones also act as shock absorbers while woodpeckers pound on wood.

All the bones in a woodpecker's skull are sturdy, to protect the brain when the bird hammers. The bone along the base of the bill is especially thick and strong. This bone also acts as a shock absorber. It and the bone inside the bill can move slightly, so there is some "give" when the bird strikes wood.

The bill itself is built for hard work. Like the bills of other birds, woodpecker bills are made of bone covered by a thick layer of horn. Horn is made of keratin, the same material that makes up human fingernails. The woodpecker's bill is long compared to the bills of most other birds. In large species, it may be more than 3 inches (7.6 cm) long. Although a woodpecker's bill is long, it is not very wide. This shape lets the bird chisel deep holes in wood. It also helps the woodpecker flip away big chunks of bark as it searches for insects to eat.

Each species of woodpecker has a bill suited for the way it finds food. Pileated woodpeckers (above) seek insects deep inside trees, while downy woodpeckers (left) probe for insects that live in cracks in the bark.

Even the woodpecker's nostrils are made for knocking on wood. These openings at the base of the bill are covered by fine, bristly feathers that keep wood chips and sawdust from getting into them.

All of these adaptations enable woodpeckers to knock on wood. Woodpeckers hammer on wood to do three very important things: communicate with each other, find food, and chisel holes in which to live and raise their young.

A red-headed woodpecker knocks on wood. Is it communicating, finding food, or building a hole in which to live and raise young?

16

Woodpeckers have many ways of communicating. In addition to hammering, as this woodpecker is doing, they also call to each other and use their wings and body posture to get their messages across.

SENDING THE MESSAGE

Woodpeckers communicate in a number of ways. Many woodpecker species make calls that are sharp and piercing, or loud and rattling. When they spread their wings, dip their heads, or fluff up the brightly colored patches of feathers on their heads, they are telling other woodpeckers who they are and what areas belong to them.

What makes woodpeckers unique is that they also tap to communicate with each other. They knock on any object, such as a hollow tree trunk, to make a loud sound. Through **drumming,** which is loud and fast, and **demonstration tapping,** which is softer and slower, woodpeckers attract mates and warn other woodpeckers to stay away. A few other kinds of birds tap and drum occasionally, but woodpeckers are the only birds who knock on wood as a main way of sending messages.

Different woodpecker species drum and tap with different speeds and rhythms. The downy woodpecker *(Picoides pubescens)* gives one long roll: tr-rrrrrrrrrrrr. The yellow-bellied sapsucker *(Sphyrapicus varius)* starts and ends with slow taps, and makes a series of faster blows in the middle: tap-tap-tr-rrrrrrrrrrrrr-tap-tap-tap-tap.

Sometimes woodpeckers, like this white-headed woodpecker (Picoides albolarvatus), *need a break from knocking.*

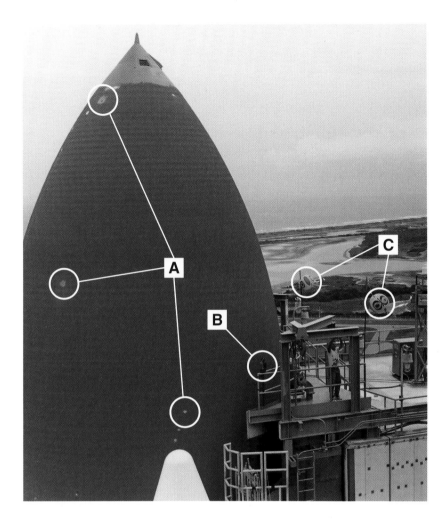

Woodpeckers have damaged many human-made structures, including the space shuttle. In 1995, flickers looking for a high, loud surface to knock on found the shuttle atop its launch pad at the John F. Kennedy Space Center in Florida an attractive target. The flickers hammered nearly two hundred holes (A) in the space shuttle's external tank. Workers frightened the flickers away from the shuttle by putting fake owls (B) and balloons with scary eyes (C) on the support tower.

Woodpeckers also differ in how much time they spend knocking on wood. In some species, both males and females drum and tap about the same amount of time. In other species, the males do more. While trying to attract a mate, a male may drum hundreds of times a day. Later, after he has won a mate and starts raising young, he drums just a few dozen times a day.

In areas that are home to more than one kind of woodpecker, the birds can recognize when their own species is doing the drumming. For example, the lesser spotted woodpecker *(Picoides minor)* and the black woodpecker *(Dryocopus martius)* live in the same areas of northern Europe and Asia. When biologists played tape recordings of one of these species drumming, only birds of the same species responded.

Like most other woodpeckers, a Nuttall's woodpecker (Picoides nuttallii) *prefers insects over other foods.*

FINDING FOOD

Almost all woodpecker species eat a variety of foods. They eat insects such as ants, flies, termites, beetles, and caterpillars. Most also eat fruits and nuts, and some eat the eggs and young of other birds. A few—the sapsuckers—tap into living trees to get at the rich, sugary sap.

Ants are the number one food for most woodpeckers around the world. The birds find adult ants on the ground, in rotting logs, and on trees. They also use their strong bills to chisel into anthills to find plump, nutritious ant **larvae** (LAR-vee), or immature ants. Biologists have found flickers that had eaten as many as five thousand ants within a few hours. Flickers' tongues are coated with lots of sticky saliva, or spit, that ants stick to. Their saliva also protects flickers against formic acid, a substance ants produce that burns the skin and digestive systems of most other animals that try to eat them.

Almost all woodpeckers get their food on or in trees. They **forage,** or look for food, in ways that few other birds do. Woodpeckers forage by starting at the base of a tree and hopping up the trunk a few inches at a time. They look for insects to eat as they spiral up and around the trunk. When they reach the top of the tree, they swoop down to the base of another tree to search its trunk. Woodpeckers sometimes cling upside-down to large tree limbs as they seek food.

As they move up a trunk or along a branch, woodpeckers use several methods to find insects to eat. The birds pick insects off the surface of the bark and leaves. Many species pry chunks of bark from dead or dying trees. This often uncovers insects that had been hiding under the bark.

A female downy pries loose a piece of bark to get to the insects hiding underneath.

21

Some woodpeckers peck hard enough to **excavate** (EKS-kuh-vayt), or chisel out, a large hole and reach insects living deep within the wood. These woodpeckers chisel into the wood to find the little tunnels where insects such as wood-boring beetles have laid their eggs. Those eggs develop into larvae, which stay inside the tunnels until they become adult beetles.

Woodpeckers seek out these nutritious prey by listening to how the wood sounds when they tap on it. Like other birds, woodpeckers have a poor sense of smell and taste, but very sharp hearing. Wood that has tunnels in it sounds more hollow than solid wood does. Woodpeckers can also sense vibrations made by larvae and other insects as they move within the wood. When woodpeckers detect insects within a tree, they hammer away with their chisel-shaped bills. They toss aside moss, bits of leaves, and chunks of dead bark as they excavate down to where their prey lie.

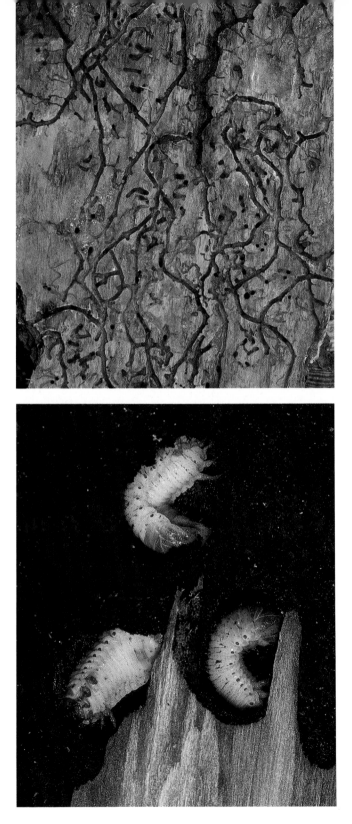

Woodpeckers excavate holes to reach tunnels created by pine bark beetles (top). The birds are searching for beetle larvae (bottom) to eat.

22

A pileated woodpecker uses its long tongue to snag larvae living under the bark of a dead tree.

Once woodpeckers locate food, their long tongues help them catch it. Woodpeckers are able to stick their tongues out farther than any other bird except hummingbirds—up to 4 inches (10 cm) past the tip of the bill! Woodpeckers that hunt for insect larvae have tongues with sharp barbs at the end. When the woodpecker sticks its long tongue down an insect tunnel, the barbs snag the soft larvae so they can be pulled out and eaten.

A few species, such as the red-headed woodpecker *(Melanerpes erythrocephalus),* catch flies and other insects in midflight. They perch on a branch and watch for the insects to fly past. Then they zoom out, nab the prey in mid-air, and return to their perch to swallow their meal.

Many woodpeckers eat insects in the warm seasons but turn to fruits and nuts as a source of food in winter, when few insects are available. For example, the acorn woodpecker *(Melanerpes formicivorus)* eats mainly ants during the warm months. As winter approaches, it stores thousands of acorns in pits it excavates in a large tree called a **granary** (GRAY-nur-ee). Each colony of acorn woodpeckers keeps a granary of its own. One such granary contained more than 30,000 holes, each with an acorn tucked snugly inside it. During winter and spring, the woodpeckers retrieve and eat the stashed acorns. The birds need their granary to survive. They guard it and pass it down from generation to generation.

A female red-bellied woodpecker feasts on berries (above). Acorn woodpeckers (below) need a big tree that they can use as a granary. Without that, members of a colony won't stay in an area even if there are plenty of oak trees and acorns available.

Sapsuckers have one of the most specialized ways of obtaining food. Each sapsucker pokes up to 30 holes each day into living trees. Sap flows out through these holes, which are called **wells.** Sapsuckers drink the sugary liquid. Their tongues have fine, hairlike barbs that make the tip of the tongue look like a paintbrush. The barbs let the sapsucker lap up lots of sap from its wells.

Sapsuckers also catch and eat insects that come to drink the sap. The birds spend a lot of time tending their wells, picking away dirt and dried sap with their bills. This keeps the wells open so the sap continues to flow freely.

Other birds benefit from sapsuckers' work as well. More than 30 species, including downy and red-bellied woodpeckers, hummingbirds, ruby-crowned kinglets, and many warblers, eat either tree sap or the insects attracted by the sap. But only sapsuckers are able to make the holes that make the sap available.

Different species of woodpeckers can live in the same area if they eat different foods. For example, downy woodpeckers hunt for insects in bushes, small trees, and the tips of branches of big trees. Hairy woodpeckers *(Picoides villosus),* which are larger and stronger than downy woodpeckers, probe for insects deep inside the trunks and branches of large trees. Since they don't compete with each other for the same foods, they can live side by side in the same forests in North America.

A red-breasted sapsucker laps up the sugary sap from one of the many wells it has excavated in this tree. Sapsuckers usually migrate to warmer regions in the winter.

AT HOME IN THE TREES

Almost all woodpeckers excavate holes to sleep in at night. These holes protect them from rain, wind, and other animals. In most species, each bird excavates a new **roost hole** for itself every year. Old holes may be dirty or have parasites in them.

Woodpeckers usually make their holes in dead trees that are still standing, called **snags.** Some species can even excavate holes in living trees, whose wood is very hard. A few kinds of woodpeckers live on the plains, or areas with tall grass. They make their roost holes in the ground rather than in trees. They choose a stream bank or another place where they can excavate sideways into the earth. Although they live on the plains, these birds—several African and South American flickers, and occasionally the common flicker of North America—use the same chiseling skills as their relatives who live in the trees.

Downy woodpeckers, which are small, often make their roost holes on the undersides of large tree limbs. Large species, like the pileated woodpecker (*Dryocopus pileatus),* may use a hole created by another woodpecker or by insects. Since pileateds are so large, they usually must expand the holes they find so they can fit inside. The Gila woodpecker (*Melanerpes uropygialis*) of the American southwest often makes its roost holes high up in saguaro cacti.

Gila woodpeckers live in a small area in the southwestern United States and in Mexico. They often build their roost holes in cacti.

A red-headed woodpecker removes wood chips to enlarge its new roost hole.

It takes most woodpeckers at least a week to excavate a roost hole. Usually the bird bores a hole that goes sideways into the trunk for a few inches and then heads downward for 8 to 12 inches (20–30 cm). The hole is just big enough to let the adult bird rest comfortably inside it, clinging upright to the inside wall.

For most species, finding large, old trees in which to make their roost holes is harder than finding enough food to eat. The red-cockaded woodpecker *(Picoides borealis)*, for example, can adjust to various kinds of insects or fruits in its diet. But it needs pine trees that are at least 80 years old in which to build its roost hole.

Red-cockaded woodpeckers are one of the few animals on earth that can excavate a hole in a living pine tree. The wood of these trees is so hard that it takes the woodpeckers six months to a year to finish a roost hole. Since it takes so long to excavate a hole, red-cockaded woodpeckers keep the same roost hole year after year instead of making a new one each year. They will even use the old hole of a woodpecker that has died.

Red-cockaded woodpeckers make their homes in very old, diseased pine trees. Diseased wood is softer and easier for woodpeckers to excavate. If the bird discovers that the tree it started to chisel into is not diseased, it abandons that tree and starts to make a hole in another one.

Owls often live in holes that have been abandoned by woodpeckers.

Woodpeckers are not the only animals that nest in holes in trees, but they are the only animals that regularly excavate the holes themselves. Squirrels, chickadees, and owls also make their homes in such holes, but they are not able to build the holes themselves. They often take over holes made by woodpeckers. For example, the abandoned holes of Gila woodpeckers become new homes for falcons, owls, wrens, lizards, or mice.

Sometimes people remove the large, old trees that woodpeckers rely on most. They clear the land to plant crops or to gain a better view from a house, or they use the wood to build things. When many potential nest trees are removed from a large area, the woodpeckers either leave the area or die off. But if people leave enough of the largest, oldest trees, the woodpeckers can stay and raise families there.

RAISING A FAMILY

Every spring, a woodpecker prepares to raise a family. First it must find a mate.

Although to us many male and female woodpeckers may look similar, other woodpeckers can easily tell them apart. Usually there is a difference in color on the head or neck. Many woodpecker species have a splash of color, called a **malar** (MAY-lar) **stripe,** at the base of their bills. A malar stripe looks like a mustache. In some species, a male's malar stripe is red, while a female's is black. In northern flickers *(Colaptes auratus),* only the male has a malar stripe. Biologists once did an experiment that showed this is how the birds tell males from females. When they painted a malar stripe on a female flicker, other flickers—even the female's own mate—acted as if she were male.

There are two types of northern flickers, the yellow-shafted and the red-shafted (shown here). They are named for the color of the wing feathers that are visible when the bird is flying. The male yellow-shafted has a black malar stripe and the male red-shafted (top) has a red malar stripe. The females of both types (red-shafted shown bottom) lack malar stripes.

Two Gila woodpeckers

When a male and a female woodpecker meet just before breeding season, each tries to show the other what a good mate he or she will be. Each species has its own way of doing this. The male and female may fly past each other to show off the colors on their wings and bellies. The female may follow the male around and chase away other females that approach him. The male may drum loudly to show the female what a good nest tree he has. He does this because his roost hole usually becomes a **nest hole,** or the hole in a tree where woodpecker parents raise their young.

31

When a male and a female choose each other as mates, they start turning the male's roost hole into a nest hole. They enlarge the bottom of it to form a chamber large enough to hold the baby birds. The mates take turns, but males usually do more of the nest-building work. While one partner excavates, the other partner stands guard and chases away woodpeckers and other kinds of animals who might try to take over the nest hole. All through the breeding season, the male continues to sleep in this hole, while the female returns to her own roost hole every night.

As they excavate, the woodpeckers let some of the wood chips and sawdust they produce fall to the bottom of the hole to form a cushion. They use their bills to carry extra material away from the nest hole. They don't put grass, twigs, or feathers in their nests as many other birds do.

A pair of red-headed woodpeckers. They probably enlarged the male's roost hole to make a nest hole for their babies.

Red-bellied woodpecker eggs

During the two or three weeks it takes them to prepare the nest hole, the two birds mate. The female crouches on a horizontal branch, and the male hops on her back. Then he slips to one side of her as the female's tail tilts to the other side. That lets their bellies come near each other. Then sperm, or male sex cells, can pass from an opening beneath the male's tail into a similar opening beneath the female's tail.

Inside the female's body, sperm **fertilizes,** or joins with, egg cells. Then the shell is put around the fertilized egg by a special part of the female's body called the shell gland. After this, the eggs are ready to be laid.

The female woodpecker begins to lay her plump, white eggs as soon as the nest hole is complete. She lays one egg per day. Woodpeckers that live in hot, tropical areas lay just 1 to 3 eggs. Woodpeckers that live in cooler regions such as North America, southern South America, and Europe, lay 6 to 11 eggs.

The size of the eggs depends on the size of the parents. The eggs of small species such as downy woodpeckers are less than an inch (25 mm) long and about half an inch (13 mm) wide. Eggs of large species such as pileated woodpeckers are about 1.3 inches (33 mm) long and an inch (25 mm) wide.

Once all the eggs are laid, the parents take turns sitting on the eggs to **incubate** them, or keep them warm so the baby woodpeckers inside will develop. The parents trade off every couple of hours during the day. In most species, the male sits on the eggs all night.

Incubation lasts 11 to 14 days in small species, and up to 21 days in large species. It ends when the baby woodpeckers hatch, or break out of their eggshells. The newly hatched babies, or **nestlings,** have just a few fuzzy feathers. Their eyes remain closed because they are not yet fully developed.

Nestlings demand a lot from their parents. Since the baby birds have few feathers, a parent must stay in the nest hole with them to keep them warm. Their parents must bring them food many times a day. Some bring chunks of fresh berries or insects for their babies to eat. Other parents eat the food first, then **regurgitate** (ree-GUR-jih-tayt), or throw up, the food when they come to the nest. The parents also clean the nest hole by carrying away the nestlings' **fecal sacs** (FEE-kuhl saks), which are little bags of feces, or droppings.

The nestlings call or chirp loudly to attract their parents' attention. Often the loudest nestling gets fed first. The parents also call to each other. They make a soft, chirping sound to tell each other where they are. They also make a harsher, louder call to tell other birds to stay away from their home. Some sound a loud, sharp cry if they spot a nearby **predator,** or an animal that hunts and eats other animals for food. Woodpecker predators are animals such as owls, hawks, squirrels, and snakes.

These baby pileated woodpeckers are resting in their nest hole (above). Even at this early age they have long, strong bills. A female northern flicker carries out a fecal sac (right).

A male three-toed woodpecker (Picoides tridactylus) *feeds one of his babies.*

As the baby woodpeckers grow, they become stronger. At about 9 days old, their eyes open and the nestlings start to develop feathers. After 3 to 5 weeks in the nest hole, they are ready to try their wings. They crowd into the entrance of the hole, watching their parents come and go. Finally, one bold youngster flies from the hole. Soon, all the young woodpeckers are fluttering around outside. Their ability to fly is an instinct, or something they are born with, rather than something they learn by watching their parents.

At first, young woodpeckers communicate with calls, chirps, and displays. They won't knock on wood to communicate until they are a few months old.

In tropical regions, young woodpeckers stay near their parents for several months. In other parts of the world, the young birds leave their parents soon after they begin to fly. They scatter to nearby areas, where they must quickly learn to find food and shelter on their own. It will be several months—nearly the beginning of winter—before they are large enough and strong enough to excavate their own roost holes. Until then, they sleep in the open, clinging to tree trunks.

Often they sleep just under a large branch. This provides some shelter from cold and rain, and helps them hide from predators.

This is the most dangerous time for the young woodpeckers. Within a few weeks of leaving their parents, most of them die of hunger or are killed by predators. In most years, only one or two of the youngsters produced by a pair of woodpeckers survive their first summer and go on to make homes of their own.

Young pileated woodpeckers crowd the entrance of their nest hole (above). *This red-headed youngster* (right) *will be ready to leave his parents soon.*

WOODPECKERS' ENEMIES

Adult woodpeckers rarely fall prey to their predators. When a woodpecker is out of its hole, its markings help it blend in with the pattern of shadows and light on tree limbs. When a woodpecker is inside its hole, it is a very tough customer. If a predator sticks its head into the hole, the woodpecker hammers it with its strong bill. Sometimes, though, a predator succeeds in killing an adult woodpecker.

Nestlings are much more likely to become dinner for a predator. Black rat snakes climb well and have been found inside woodpecker nest holes 60 feet (18 m) above the ground, eating whole families of nestlings. If a parent is in the nest hole, it can protect the nestlings. But if both parents are away from the nest in search of food, it is easier for predators to enter the nest hole and eat the babies.

The black rat snake is a common predator of woodpecker nestlings. Its ability to climb trees makes it a dangerous enemy for many woodpecker species.

Sometimes animals such as flying squirrels take over holes that woodpeckers were still using.

Red-cockaded woodpeckers have an unusual way of protecting their babies against snakes. They nest in holes in large, old pine trees, and they peel the bark away from the trunk around their nest hole. This lets pine pitch ooze out. Pitch is a thick, gooey, strong-smelling substance. A snake cannot cross that sticky area. Pine pitch seems to irritate a snake and also gums up the scales on its belly so it becomes almost paralyzed.

The main problem adult woodpeckers face is finding and keeping good nest and roost holes. Sometimes other animals, such as squirrels, bluebirds, starlings, and owls, take over holes that woodpeckers are still using. Or larger woodpeckers may chase smaller woodpeckers away and enlarge the holes for their own use. Then the woodpeckers must start building a new hole all over again, which takes time and energy. If this happens during the breeding season, the woodpeckers may not have enough time to lay eggs and raise a family. If this happens in autumn, they may not have time to find a snug, safe place to roost during the winter.

Other wild animals are not the only creatures woodpeckers compete with. More than half a dozen species of woodpeckers in many places around the world are fighting to survive because of human actions. Millions of the large, old trees woodpeckers rely on for food and shelter are cut down every year to make room for farms, houses, and shopping centers, or to provide lumber.

When their habitats disappear, woodpeckers can't survive. Even if they can find enough food to live on, without big trees, they can't build nest holes. That means they can't raise families. Over a few years, the older woodpeckers die. Without youngsters to take their place, the population shrinks until finally it may disappear completely.

Loggers cut down millions of trees in which woodpeckers could build their roost holes.

The artist John James Audubon created this painting of ivory-billed woodpeckers in the early 1800s. Since then, this woodpecker has most likely become extinct.

Because their habitats are being destroyed, several species of woodpeckers have become **endangered** in the twentieth century. This means that the entire species is very close to dying out, or becoming **extinct.** When a species is extinct, it is lost forever.

The Imperial woodpecker *(Campephilus principalis),* weighing about 1.5 pounds (680 grams), was the largest woodpecker ever known. Imperial woodpeckers once lived in pine forests in the mountains of northwestern Mexico. When those forests were cut down, the great birds retreated to areas that were not very good homes for them. As the areas where they could live continued to shrink, Imperial woodpeckers gradually disappeared. Nobody has seen one since the 1950s. Many biologists believe they are extinct.

41

Another large species, the pileated woodpecker, struggled for many years. In the 1800s, as forests across eastern North America were cleared to make room for farms and cities, the species disappeared from much of the region. When some of the forests were allowed to grow back, the pileated woodpeckers returned. Since the 1920s they have become more abundant, and they are no longer in danger.

A pileated woodpecker

Some red-cockaded woodpeckers live in a pine forest on the Bates Hill Plantation in South Carolina (main). *A red-cockaded woodpecker flies to its nest hole* (inset).

Large species such as the Imperial and pileated woodpeckers need vast areas in which to hunt and raise their young—hundreds of acres of forest per pair. But smaller woodpeckers that live in colonies also need lots of room. They need enough space and food for many birds to live together. One such species is the red-cockaded woodpecker, one of the most famous endangered birds in the United States. These birds live in colonies of up to 10 birds. Each bird in the colony has its own roost hole, so the group must have not just one good tree, but several. A good tree is one that is at least 80 years old, so it is large enough to hold a roost or nest hole. Each colony needs at least 200 acres (81 hectares) of old pine forest in order to survive.

Red-cockaded woodpeckers once lived in pine forests throughout the southeastern United States, from Texas to the Atlantic coast, and from Florida to Arkansas and Virginia. These days, they live in just a few areas where pine forests still exist, such as on military bases, power plants, and wildlife refuges. These woodpeckers are thriving in the Appalachicola National Forest in Florida, at the United States Army's Fort Polk in Louisiana, and at the Savannah River Power Plant in South Carolina.

Some people have said that red-cockaded woodpeckers kill the trees in which they build their roost holes. They think the woodpeckers bring bacteria and fungi into the trees through the holes they make. This is not true. Scientists who studied thousands of trees found that tree disease had nothing to do with whether or not woodpeckers had hammered into them.

Many of the insects woodpeckers eat, such as wood-boring beetles, bark beetles, and coddling moths, damage trees or fruit in forests and orchards. Both of these photographs show beetle damage to trees. Woodpeckers help protect the trees by consuming thousands of destructive insects every day.

Red-cockaded woodpeckers play an important role in the forest community. Many animals who can't excavate holes themselves—such as flying squirrels, red-headed woodpeckers, flickers, flycatchers, and even honeybees—make their nests in old holes of red-cockaded woodpeckers. These other animals have trouble finding homes if the red-cockaded woodpeckers aren't around to create holes in trees.

Can the red-cockaded woodpecker survive? Will it rebound, like the pileated woodpecker? Or will it disappear from the earth forever, like the Imperial woodpecker?

The best way that we can help red-cockaded and other kinds of woodpeckers is to leave enough woods with large, old trees where they can make homes. If we do that, these fascinating birds—and all the other animals that depend on them—have a good chance to survive.

GLOSSARY

adaptation: a change that enables a plant or animal to survive in a specific environment

colony: a group of the same kind of animal living together

demonstration tapping: soft, slow tapping made by a woodpecker to communicate with other woodpeckers

drumming: loud, fast tapping made by a woodpecker to communicate with other woodpeckers

endangered: at risk of losing all members of a type of plant or animal forever

excavate: to chisel out

extinct: when no members of a species are left alive

fecal sac: small bundle of droppings produced by a baby woodpecker

fertilization: the joining of a sperm from the male and an egg from the female to produce a baby

forage: to look for food

granary: a large tree in which acorn woodpeckers store thousands of acorns to eat during the winter months

habitat: the kind of environment in which a plant or animal normally lives. A habitat includes the kinds of plants and animals that live in it, the type of soil and water it has, and its climate.

incubate: to keep eggs warm so the baby birds inside them will develop

larvae: immature insects

malar stripe: a splash of color on the side of a woodpecker's face that resembles a mustache

nest hole: a hole in a tree in which a pair of woodpeckers raises its young

nestling: a baby bird, from the time it hatches out of its egg until it leaves the nest

Picidae: the scientific name for the woodpecker family

predator: an animal that hunts and eats other animals for food

roost hole: a hole in a tree in which a woodpecker sleeps at night

snag: a dead tree that is still standing. Woodpeckers often make their nests and roost holes in snags.

species: a particular kind of animal or plant

well: a hole hammered into a tree by a sapsucker. Sap flows out through the well, and the sapsucker (and other birds and insects) eats the sap.

INDEX

ABOUT THE AUTHOR

Richard Alan Hannon

Author **Cherie Winner** once lived in a house in the Ohio woods where she could see and hear flickers and downy, hairy, red-bellied, and pileated woodpeckers, all on the same day. The rattling call of the pileated woodpeckers became one of her favorite sounds in the whole world. She now lives in Wyoming, where she enjoys watching flickers and downies with her dog Sheba and her cat Smudge.